LIFE
LESSONS
for COUPLES

CINDY FRANCIS
AUTHOR OF ***LIFE LESSONS FOR WOMEN***

Newport House

Newport House, Inc.
107 R.R. 620 S.,
Suite 7-A
Austin, TX 78734

Life Lessons for Couples/ Cindy Francis
First Newport House edition, 1993

Cover design by Gayle Smith
Page design by Linda Wells
Typsetting and editorial assistance by Max Reshetnikov

Manufactured in the United States of America

ISBN 0-939515-49-0

For

Aunt Sarah and Uncle Irwin

*who, after 44 years of marriage,
still treat each other
like newlyweds.*

Introduction

It has always interested me that the happy and unhappy couples I know both have, generally speaking, the same problems. The happy couples aren't richer or better looking or smarter. They just do things differently. And they've learned some lessons that have helped them to have a better life together.

This little book is designed to teach you what they do and what they've learned.

Since the publication of my previous books, *Life Lessons for Women* and *Life Lessons for Mothers*, many of you have asked me to write a book specifically for couples. I've been greatly helped in this by a "success journal" I've kept for some time in which I've written what I've learned from my own marriage and from life.

I have also been helped by a number of happily married friends and relatives and by numerous marriage counselors who were kind enough to share their thoughts. In addition, I have read lots of books and journals to learn the valuable lessons they have to teach.

Here, then, are my lessons for couples. I hope you'll enjoy them, and more importantly, I hope you'll put them to use in your own relationship. I wish you lots of joy and lots of love.

LIFE
LESSONS
for COUPLES

Show your love by *listening*.

Don't wait until Friday night to be loving- be loving *all* the time!

Accept each other as you are.

Be your partner's best friend.

Respect each other-- and show it
by treating each other with respect.

Help without being asked.

Words your partner would like to hear more often:

"I have faith in you."

"I love you."

"You did a fine job."

"Thank you."

Appreciate what you have.

Make time to be alone
with each other.

Cuddle early in the evening,
before you're too tired.

If what you're doing isn't working, try something else.

Look for win/win solutions.

You can always make more money, but you can never make more time. Take time *now* for your family.

When you need help, speak up!

It's not enough just to say ''I love you.'' *Live your love* by being considerate and kind.

Leave your job- and it's problems- at the office.

Love has good manners.

At parties, pay more attention to your partner than to anyone else.

If you are having problems, figure out first the role *you* are playing.

Always make your partner feel special.

Give more love and
you'll get more love.

If you're not sure whether
to say something, don't.

*Kindness is
love in action.*

Share your feelings.

Call during the day, just
to say "I love you."

50/50 isn't enough. You each
have to give 100% if you want
to have a *great* relationship.

Turn the TV off and take
time to talk together.

You're part of a couple, but
be your own person as well.

Picture yourself as older, looking
back on your life together. What do
you wish you had done? *Do it now.*

If you're not happy,
negotiate for change.

Say positive affirmations about
each other and your relationship.

Make having fun together a priority.

Keep courting each other after marriage.

Never go to bed mad.

Your sweetheart needs touching and affection in *and out* of the bedroom.

Always take each other's feelings into consideration.

Kiss each other every night
before turning out the lights.

Plan together for the future, and then
work to make your plans come true.

Treat your partner at least as
well as you treat your friends.

Keep up with your individual hopes and dreams.

Brag about each other.

If your mate's always busy, make appointments to see each other.

When your partner tells you a problem, don't rush in with a solution. Often they just want to be *heard*.

Pay attention to how often you interrupt and do it less.

Turn up the stereo and
practice slow dancing.

Be loving, even when you
don't feel particularly loving.

When discussions get too
hot, call "Time Out."

Bring home flowers
to your sweetheart.

View the problems life gives you as
challenges to be faced together.

It's okay to change your mind.

When you're conversing, give your undivided attention.

It takes 72 muscles to frown and only 23 to smile- and smiling has *much* more pleasurable results!

Your time and attention are the most important gifts you can give.

Expect changes in your relationship-
and work to make them positive.

Visualize a bright future
for the two of you.

Give gifts which reflect your special
knowledge of your partner.

Assure your partner
often that you care.

Let your mate know you
care by how you act.

Look for what's good in
your partner and praise it.

Support each other's growth.

When your partner comes home,
drop what you're doing and give
a big welcome at the door.

Your partner will only satisfy *some* of
your needs. Look to others for the rest.

Make Valentine's Day -
Valentine's <u>Week</u>!

If you want your mate to understand
you, talk about yourself more.

Hinting hardly ever works.
The best way to get what
you want is to ask for it.

To encourage your mate to talk:
As you're listening, ask yourself,
"What is he feeling?" "What is he saying?"
Then answer whichever question seems
more important. ("You sound upset.")
Let your partner correct you or
confirm that you got it right.

For Every Day's "To Do" List:

☐ Talk   ☐ Kiss and hug

☐ Listen   ☐ Compliment

☐ Help out   ☐ Express your love

Honesty is important,
but be tactful.

Assure your partner you'll
always be there.

Spend more time with other couples
with whom you can laugh and joke.

Write little love notes and leave them...

- on the driver's seat
- in the refrigerator, taped to a favorite food
- on the pillow
- inside your mate's purse or wallet

Try roller skating together!

Get your partner talking by asking
about a hobby or sport that's of interest.

One evening, hire a student who plays
the violin to perform, while the two of
you enjoy a candlelight dinner!

Cuddle in a drive-in movie.

Show you're on your partner's side.

Give up trying to control the other person. The only person you can really ever control is *you*.

Get up early and watch the sunrise.

When criticism is true, agree with it. ("You're right. I am late.")

Share your fantasies!

Be honest with each other.

During tough times, think of
why you fell in love in the first
place. Dwell on those things.

"I love you" are the words your partner most wants to hear.

You can disagree without
being disagreeable.

Treat each other in an
"I'm OK - You're OK" manner.

When you feel angry, cool
down before you speak up.

Express appreciation for favors.

Touch more. Touching often expresses sentiments that words alone can't convey.

Volunteer together to help a favorite charity.

Base your relationship on *your commitment to each other*, not on your feelings of love. That way, as your feelings for each other rise and fall- as they surely will- your relationship will still be secure.

Instead of arguing,
do problem solving.

Cuddle while you watch TV.

When your partner makes a
mistake, don't say "I told you so."

Surprise your mate with
a spontaneous kiss.

Take dance lessons together.

Every once in a while,
baby each other!

Just because you're angry
doesn't mean you're right.

When something goes wrong, instead
of assessing blame, focus on how to do
better next time.

*Set aside time
to be loving.*

Play *Enchanted Evening*, a romantic game for couples.

Treat each other the way you want to be treated.

It's easier in the long run to face your responsibilities.

Do what makes your partner
feel loved. If you don't
know what that is, ask.

Tell your partner when
you need extra attention.

Give a back rub without being asked.

Cherish each other.

Cut out articles that are likely to interest your partner.

Buy tickets, but don't say for what. The waiting and the surprise will be almost as much fun as the event.

Read *You Just Don't Understand: Women and Men in Conversation* to learn better ways to communicate.

Give your mate ''Love Coupons'' good for flowers, kisses, massages, etc.

Be an encourager!

What your partner needs most:

Appreciation Understanding
Admiration   Love
Acceptance   To be cherished
Encouragement To be cared for

Make decisions when you're calm, never when you're angry.

Let your mate know it's safe to tell you everything.

Give lots of hugs.

View your mate as a companion to enjoy life with- not a possession to ignore.

When you feel short-changed, examine whether you have unrealistic expectations.

Be on the lookout for
ways to make life more fun.

Write a poem. It doesn't
have to be good- it just has
to have your feelings in it.

Focus on what's *right,*
not who's *right.*

Try out new restaurants.

Rather than give good advice,
set a good example.

Put a dimmer on your
bedroom light switch.

Some people express love by working hard. Let them know you understand that.

Cook your sweetheart's favorite meal.

Share what life was like when you were children.

Watch 30's romances together.
Anything by Fred Astaire and
Ginger Rogers will do fine.

Be grateful for your partner's love.
(Remember when you didn't have it?)

Take vacations often, even if just
one night at a bed and breakfast.

List all the ways your partner
enriches your life. Share your list.

Don't make sex the last
item on your "to do" list.

To see each other's point of view,
role-play being the other person.

Be tolerant. You're both
fallible human beings.

Find something to like about
each other's friends.

*Nurture the child
in your partner.*

Exercise together.

Help your partner fulfill
personal goals.

View money as belonging to you
both, no matter who made it.

More words your partner would like to hear more often:

"You can do it!"

"You're looking good."

"How can I help?"

"I'm proud of you!"

Earn more
than you spend.

Respect the fact that your love's needs
and wants may differ from yours.

Honor each other's differences
rather than trying to change them.

Rent a rowboat and enjoy a romantic hour on the lake.

Save for tomorrow, but don't go completely without today.

Be action-oriented. Instead of *waiting* for things to happen, work to *make* them happen!

Read the wonderful "Love" chapter in *The Road Less Traveled* for a realistic assessment of love and what it requires of us.

Go through objects each of you has saved from the past. Talk about why they're special to you.

Trust each other
& be worthy of trust.

Judge each other with compassion, not by a standard of perfection.

If both of you have jobs, it's only fair that you both share the housework. Work out a specific agreement as to who does what.

Have a "date night" once a week.

Flirt more.

Consideration and kindness *out of bed* help promote good feelings *in bed.*

See the opportunities
inside problems.

Hold hands.

Mark anniversaries and birthdays
on your datebook and calendar.
That way you won't forget.

Let your partner unwind
after a long day. Bring up
problems *after* dinner.

Instead of confronting each other on
opposite sides of the table, learn to share
the same side of the table and confront
your problems on the other side.

Fighting Fair - Do's

Take turns talking.

Bring up only *one* problem at a time.

Focus on the present.

Express how you feel.

Restate each others' points to their satisfaction before voicing your own opinions.

Fighting Fair - Don'ts

Interrupt

Label each other, their behavior or ideas

Threaten

Tell each other their motives
 ("You deliberately...")

Shout, swear or hit

Write down things you have been
happiest doing together in the past.
Do those things more often.

Be close, but always keep
some space for yourself.

Learn to forgive.

Respect the privacy of each other's purse, wallet, papers and mail.

Once in a while, each of you have a day which is "yours." On that day, you get treated extra nice and get to choose what both of you will do.

Make your own birthday, anniversary, New Year's, and Valentine's Day cards- and write out how *you* feel.

Even if it's not a holiday, write a love note to your sweetheart.

Learn to make *yourself* happy
instead of relying on your partner.

Bike ride together in the countryside.

Learn some foreign words and
phrases, so you'll have a ''secret''
language the two of you can use.

Meet problems
together head on.

Look for the brightest
star and make a wish.

Turn your weaknesses into strengths by
filling in where each other is lacking.

Start a hobby together.

Realize you both want the same
things: to love and be loved, to
contribute and be appreciated,
to have fun, and to feel secure.

Asking for help doesn't mean you're weak- just intelligent.

Take a bath together, complete with jasmine scented bath oils, scented candles, and soft music.

If you care,
speak in a caring way.

Overlook each other's flaws-
remembering that you have your own.

Share your dreams.

Don't take each other for granted.

There is no perfect love
out there waiting for you.
Enjoy the one you have.

When you hurt your
partner, say you're sorry.

Dress up for each other.

Criticize only in private.

When you present a gift,
wrap it beautifully. Your
effort will be appreciated.

You may not always agree, but
always hear each other out.

You teach each other how to treat you. If you refuse to accept bad treatment, it'll stop.

Never assume marriage will change either of you.

You can make mistakes and still be OK.

Avoid comparing yourselves with other couples. You'll never know the truth about them, and it's wiser to just enjoy your own happiness.

Humor is healing- and it's fun too!

Get a guidebook for your area, and explore the places you haven't yet visited.

Put each other before all others, including your parents and friends.

When things go wrong, accept
your part of the responsibility .

Show you're open to
conversation by keeping your
legs and arms uncrossed.

Buy gifts that say, "I love you"-
no pots and pans.

To be interesting,
be interested.

Admire each other's achievements.

Thank your partner for
compliments and kind gestures-
and you'll get more of them!

Not *all* your mate's problems are *your* problems. Sometimes it's better to be uninvolved.

Have your partner be your best friend- not your only friend.

Play tennis or Ping-Pong together.

Nurture and protect the things
you love about your partner.

Ask yourself how you can add to
your relationship, instead of
what more you can get from it.

Never bring up past loves.

''Peace at any Price'' leads to
temporary peace at a high price.
Better to work things out.

Spend your energy fixing problems
rather than assigning blame.

Have a love affair with your mate.

There is no perfect harmony
in marriage, only a series of
adjustments.

Use things, not people.
Love people, not things.

Recognize each other's
contributions to the family.

Surprise your partner
with breakfast in bed.

Give your love
unconditionally.

Take time for yourself too.

Happy marriages come from balanced exchanges.

If you feel resentful, start asking for what you want more.

If you feel guilty, start giving more.

Give more massages.

Go on lots of walks
together, arm-in-arm.

Thank your partner for
doing household chores.

Keep your promises.

Be faithful.

Go to bed early and
talk in the dark.

Buy frivolous things for your partner
that she wouldn't buy for herself.

Propose a toast to your mate, even though you've only got water in your glass!

Write each other a note saying how the other person has changed your life for the better.

When you're angry, *think* before you speak.

View things that go wrong as "unfortunate"- not horrible. Most of what we "awfulize" about, we won't even remember in a few days.

*Focus on the
90% that's right-
not the 10% that isn't.*

Have a professional photo
taken of the two of you.

Your relationship is like a bank
account: you have to put into it
before you can take out of it.

Cuddle often, even when you don't want sex.

Take in more live theater.

The time you spend counts far more than the money you spend.

Keep a scrapbook of your
favorite moments together.
Look through it on rainy days.

If expressing your feelings is
hard for you, write them out.

*Set aside time
for romance.*

Let your partner know
you find her attractive.

It's okay to disagree.

When your mate comes home from
a trip, put up a poster saying,
"WELCOME HOME!"

Reaffirm your vows in front
of your friends and family.

Develop common goals.

Take the phone off the hook
during intimate moments.

Ask more open-ended questions.

They begin with "how," "why," and "tell me about"- and they encourage your partner to open up.
("Tell me about the highlight of your day." "Why are you so eager to see the exhibit?")

Don't ask too open-ended questions.

They ask for *so* much information, all
you get are one or two word answers.
*("Tell me all about your day."
"What's new at work?")*

Be outrageous once in a while.

The best way to encourage
your partner to change is
to change yourself.

Your first task is to manage your own life.

Flatter your partner.

When your mate's almost done bathing, sneak the towel out of the bathroom- and warm it in the dryer!

Have priorities,
& make love first-
not last.

Your feelings come from your thinking.
If you change your thoughts about your
mate, your feelings will change.

> Instead of criticizing
> what you don't like,
> praise what you do like.

Tackle problems early, while they're small, while there are still lots of good feelings.

Write out together 10 things you'd love to do together. Then, get started doing them!

*Always take
care of each other.*

Other books by Cindy Francis:

Life Lessons for Women

Life Lessons for Mothers